±1

⑭6

KT-161-874

# low fat

# low fat

This edition first published in the U.K. in 1999 by Hamlyn for WHSmith, Greenbridge Road, Swindon SN3 3LD

Octopus Publishing Group Limited
2–4 Heron Quays
London E14 4JP

ISBN 0 600 59890 X

Printed in China

## Notes

**1** Standard level spoon measurements are used in all recipes.

1 tablespoon = one 15 ml spoon
1 teaspoon = one 5 ml spoon

**2** Both imperial and metric measurements have been given in all recipes. Use one set of measurements only and not a mixture of both.

**3** Measurements for canned food have been given as a standard metric equivalent.

**4** Eggs should be medium unless otherwise stated. The Department of Health advises that eggs should not be consumed raw. This book may contain dishes made with lightly cooked eggs. It is prudent for more vulnerable people, such as pregnant and nursing mothers, invalids, the elderly, babies and young children, to avoid uncooked or lightly cooked dishes made with eggs. Once prepared, these dishes should be used immediately.

**5** Poultry should be cooked thoroughly. To test if poultry is cooked, pierce the flesh through the thickest part with a skewer or fork – the juices should run clear, never pink or red.

**6** Fresh herbs should be used unless otherwise stated. If unavailable, use dried herbs as an alternative but halve the quantities stated.

**7** Pepper should be freshly ground black pepper unless otherwise stated; season according to taste.

**8** Ovens should be preheated to the specified temperature – if using a fan-assisted oven, follow the manufacturer's instructions for adjusting the time and the temperature.

**9** Do not refreeze a dish that has been frozen previously.

**10** This book includes dishes made with nuts and nut derivatives. It is advisable for customers with known allergic reactions to nuts and nut derivatives and those who may be potentially vulnerable to these allergies, such as pregnant and nursing mothers, invalids, the elderly, babies and children, to avoid dishes made with nuts and nut oils. It is also prudent to check the labels of pre-prepared ingredients for the possible inclusion of nut derivatives.

**11** Vegetarians should look for the 'V' symbol on a cheese to ensure it is made with vegetarian rennet. There are vegetarian forms of Parmesan, feta, Cheddar, Cheshire, red Leicester, dolcelatte and many goats' cheeses, among others.

**12** All recipes in this book have been analysed by a professional nutritionist, so that you can see their nutritional content at a glance.

The abbreviations are as follows:
kcal = calories;
kJ = kilojoules;
CHO = carbohydrate.

**The analysis refers to each portion.**
Ingredients given as optional are not included in the analysis.

Whether your fancy is a warming
soup or a light summery salad,
mouth-watering kebabs, richly topped
pancakes, or simply something
vegetarian, you are sure to find a
deliciously satisfying recipe here.

The world is your oyster now, for these
recipes bring a cornucopia of tasty
ingredients from China, India, Europe
and the Americas. You will find many
favourites here, from oriental sweet
and sour dishes and stir-fries to pasta
dishes full of Mediterranean warmth.

Make the simplest meal memorable
with a main dish from this exciting
collection. It's the clever combination
of mouthwatering ingredients that
gives the recipes their special appeal:
three zesty herbs in a pasta sauce, for
instance, or turkey breasts with a
cranberry-based glaze. And they are all
wonderfully quick and easy to make.

Who would have thought low-fat
desserts and sweet things could be so
good – and so varied! The recipes here
are quite irresistible: pears with a
chocolate sauce, peaches baked with
spices, a superb berry-filled summer
pudding, and lots more. Your only
difficulty is in making a choice.

# contents

# introduction

This is a low-fat, not a no-fat cookbook. Although it is well recognized that many people would feel and be rather healthier if the amount of fat in their diets were to be cut down, it is also important to remember that we all need some dietary fat to keep our bodies performing well. For this reason, all the recipes here, while offering a wide range of delicious, good-looking dishes to suit all tastes and seasons, have been carefully balanced to include no more than 9 g of fat per serving.

## Low-fat shopping

Cutting down on the fat in our diets begins with the weekly shopping list. Keep off the list cakes, biscuits, ice creams, chips, crisps, snack and 'junk' foods or made-up dishes that require cooking in quantities of fats, such as olive oil, lard or dripping. Avoid large quantities of red meat, of which lamb is the highest in fat, and of high-fat dairy foods.

Instead, make sure the shopping trolley contains plenty of fresh vegetables, including green leafy vegetables and root vegetables, fresh fruit, lean meat, such as beef steak and pork fillet, poultry, fish, whole grains and cereals.

Low-fat dairy products to concentrate on include:

• Semi-skimmed and skimmed milk instead of full fat milk (remembering that small children should always have plenty of full fat milk because of the essential body-building fats it contains). If you find skimmed milk too watery, fortify it with skimmed milk powder for extra body and nutrition; you will find instructions on how much skimmed milk powder to use on the packet.

• Medium- and low-fat cheeses, such as quark, ricotta (a good substitute for crème fraîche, whipping cream and mascarpone) and fromage frais, which is an excellent replacement for all kinds of cream: try fresh strawberries with fromage frais just once, and you will never want to eat strawberries with cream again! Low-fat or half-fat versions of cheeses such as Cheddar and mozzarella are also more widely available.

• Low-fat and very low-fat natural yogurt. Very low-fat yogurt, which many people find rather thin, can be made as thick as higher-in-fat Greek yogurt simply by draining it through a muslin-lined sieve.

• Low-fat spreads made with all vegetable fat, which, while still far from fat-free, do contain monounsaturated fats, while most margarines contain potentially more harmful saturated animal fats.

## Using oil in low-fat cooking

Many of the recipes in this book include oil, especially vegetable oil. Good vegetable oils to use include sunflower, safflower and soya oil; these are high in polyunsaturated fats, which, in small amounts, are an essential part of a healthy diet (fish oils contain a form of polyunsaturated fat which is particularly good). Olive oil, used for its wonderful flavour, contains monounsaturated fats.

'"How long does getting thin take?"
asked Pooh anxiously.'

A. A. Milne *Winnie the Pooh*

For people wishing to reduce the fat content of their cooking to even less than the modest 9 g per serving on which this book is based, the commercial oil-sprays now widely available are ideal. The oil is mixed with water and sold in spray cans. One or two quick squirts are enough to oil a pan so that food will not stick to it during cooking. An oil-spray would be useful for cooking the Griddled Asparagus on page 24, for instance, if you were reluctant to cook it entirely dry but wished to avoid the full amount of oil given in the recipe.

Remember, too, that the amounts of oil needed in cooking can be considerably reduced if you use nonstick pans, including woks, frying pans, grill pans and omelette pans, and other utensils.

**Low-fat stocks**

Stocks are a basic ingredient in many recipes in this book. It is best to avoid stock cubes in low-fat cooking, since they are quite high in fat and generally contain too much salt. While many supermarkets now sell a good range of very acceptable fresh stocks, home-made stocks are the ideal, since you know exactly what ingredients they contain. Here are three excellent low-fat stocks, based on vegetables, chicken and fish, as well as a very useful herb seasoning which adds flavour without increasing fat content.

# vegetable stock

3 potatoes, peeled and chopped

1 onion, thinly sliced

2 leeks, split and chopped

2 celery sticks, chopped

2 carrots, chopped

1 small fennel head, thinly sliced

thyme sprigs

parsley stalks

2 bay leaves

1.5 litres (2½ pints) water

salt and pepper

Put all the ingredients, except the salt and pepper, in a large saucepan. Bring to the boil slowly, skimming off any surface scum. Add salt and pepper to taste, cover the pan and simmer for about 1½ hours, skimming the stock 3 or 4 times during cooking. Cool the stock slightly and strain through clean muslin or a very fine sieve. Finish cooling quickly and store in the refrigerator until required.

**Makes** about 1 litre (1¾ pints)

# chicken stock

1.5 kg (3 lb) chicken

2.5 litres (4 pints) water

1 bouquet garni

1 small onion, stuck with 3 cloves

1 small bunch tarragon

salt and pepper

Put the chicken and water into a large saucepan and bring slowly to the boil, skimming off any surface scum. Add the remaining ingredients, bring the pan back to the boil, lower the heat and cover the pan. Simmer gently for 1½ hours, skimming regularly. Strain the stock through clean muslin or a very fine sieve. Cool quickly and put in the refrigerator to cool completely. Remove all hardened fat from the surface of the stock before using it.

**Makes** about 1 litre (1¾ pints)

# fish stock

1 kg (2 lb) fish trimmings

1 small onion, finely chopped

2 leeks, split and chopped

1 bay leaf

parsley stalks

fennel sprigs

lemon rind

1.2 litres (2 pints) water

200 ml (7 fl oz) dry white wine

salt and pepper

Put all the ingredients, except the wine and salt and pepper, in a large saucepan. Bring slowly to the boil, skimming off any surface scum. Add the wine and salt and pepper to taste and simmer gently for 30 minutes, skimming the stock once or twice during cooking. Strain the stock through clean muslin or a fine sieve, cool quickly and store in the refrigerator until required.

**Makes** about 1 litre (1¾ pints)

# lemon herb seasoning

4½ tablespoons dried basil

4 tablespoons dried oregano

1 tablespoon pepper

1½ tablespoons dried onion

½ tablespoon whole celery seeds

½ teaspoon grated lemon rind

½ teaspoon dried garlic

Place all the ingredients in a bowl. Toss gently with a spoon until well blended. Store in an airtight container in a cool dry dark place for up to 6 months.

**Makes** about 1 jar

bean & mushroom soup •

chilled prawn & cucumber soup •

consommé with pasta •

spinach soup •

tomato & courgette soup •

pea & mint soup •

honey carrots •

medley of spring vegetables •

bean sprout salad •

tomato & vegetable kebabs •

griddled asparagus •

aubergine & red pepper layer toasts •

warm salad of turkey, red pepper & lemon •

smoked salmon pancakes •

seafood salad •

pasta, cucumber & radish salad •

pasta slaw •

# small
# courses

# bean & mushroom soup

1 Place the haricot and red kidney beans in separate saucepans, cover with cold water and bring to the boil. Boil vigorously for 10 minutes, lower the heat and simmer the haricot beans for 1½ hours and the kidney beans for 1 hour or until tender, adding salt towards the end of cooking.

2 Heat the oil in a large saucepan, add the onion and cook gently for about 5 minutes until soft. Add the garlic, mushrooms, vegetable stock and broad beans and season to taste with salt and pepper. Simmer for 10 minutes. Stir in the pasta and the drained haricot and red kidney beans and simmer for a further 15 minutes or until the pasta is just tender.

■ Canned haricot and red kidney beans make an excellent time-saving replacement for dried and soaked beans. Tip them from the can into a sieve and rinse under cold running water before adding them, well drained, with the pasta to the soup.

125 g (4 oz) dried haricot beans, soaked overnight and drained

125 g (4 oz) dried red kidney beans, soaked overnight and drained

2 tablespoons vegetable oil

1 onion, sliced

1 garlic clove, crushed

125 g (4 oz) button mushrooms, sliced

1.2 litres (2 pints) Vegetable Stock (see page 8)

175 g (6 oz) broad beans, shelled

50 g (2 oz) dried pasta, such as spirals or rings

salt and pepper

| |
|---|
| **Serves 6** |
| **Preparation time:** 15 minutes |
| **Cooking time:** about 2¼ hours, plus soaking |
| kcal 227; kJ 962; protein 15 g; fat 5 g; CHO 33 g |

# chilled prawn & cucumber soup

1 Cut the cucumber in half lengthways and scoop out and discard the seeds. Dice the flesh, reserving a few dice for the garnish.

2 Put the cucumber in a liquidizer or food processor with all the remaining ingredients except the vegetable stock and blend until smooth. Gradually whisk in the stock, then cover and chill for 1 hour.

3 Serve the soup in chilled bowls topped with ice cubes and garnished with the reserved diced cucumber and some dill sprigs.

½ cucumber, peeled

250 g (8 oz) cooked peeled prawns

4 spring onions, chopped

125 g (4 oz) ripe tomatoes, skinned, deseeded and chopped

2 tablespoons dry sherry

2 tablespoons chopped dill

½ x 200 ml (7 fl oz) carton half-fat crème fraîche

15 g (½ oz) ground almonds, toasted

1 tablespoon lime juice

1 teaspoon chilli sauce

450 ml (¾ pint) cold Vegetable Stock (see page 8)

salt and pepper

## To Garnish:

ice cubes

reserved diced cucumber

dill sprigs

**Serves 4**

**Preparation time:** 15 minutes, plus chilling

**kcal** 117; **kJ** 492; **protein** 16 g; **fat** 4 g; **CHO** 4 g

# consommé with pasta

1 Put all the ingredients, except the pasta and 4 sprigs of parsley, into a large saucepan and add enough water to come three-quarters of the way up the side of the pan. Bring to the boil and simmer over a very low heat for about 3 hours, topping up with more boiling water if the level falls below that of the meat.

2 Remove the chicken and beef from the pan and strain the consommé through a fine sieve into a bowl. Leave the soup to stand overnight and when it is completely cold skim all the fat off the surface.

3 Return the strained consommé to a saucepan, bring to the boil and add the pasta. Cook for 10–12 minutes until the pasta is just tender. Finely chop the reserved parsley. Garnish the consommé with the parsley and serve.

2 carrots, sliced

1 celery stick, halved

1 potato, halved

1 ripe tomato, halved

1 onion, halved

small bunch of parsley

500 g (1 lb) chicken pieces, skin removed

400 g (13 oz) brisket of beef

1 teaspoon salt

375 g (12 oz) dried anellini or capellini pasta

**Serves 4**

**Preparation time:** about 30 minutes, plus chilling

**Cooking time:** 3¼ hours

kcal 214; kJ 910; protein 8 g; fat 1 g; CHO 46 g

# spinach soup

1 Heat the butter or margarine in a heavy-based saucepan. Add the onion and cook over a moderate heat until soft. Add the spinach and cook until soft, stirring constantly.

2 Pour the stock into the pan and add the potato, lemon juice, nutmeg and salt and pepper to taste. Cook, partially covered, over a moderate heat for 10–12 minutes, or until the potatoes are soft.

3 Cool the mixture slightly, then purée it in a food processor or liquidizer until it is a smooth purée. Pour into a clean saucepan. Add the milk and heat the soup gently, without boiling. Transfer to warmed soup bowls and serve.

25 g (1 oz) butter or margarine

1 onion, chopped

250 g (8 oz) fresh or frozen spinach, defrosted if frozen

600 ml (1 pint) Vegetable Stock (see page 8)

1 medium potato, peeled and thinly sliced

1 teaspoon lemon juice

pinch of grated nutmeg

100 ml (3½ fl oz) semi-skimmed milk

salt and white pepper

| Serves 8 |
| --- |
| **Preparation time:** 10 minutes |
| **Cooking time:** 20 minutes |
| **kcal** 67; **kJ** 279; **protein** 4 g; **fat** 3 g; **CHO** 8 g |

# tomato & courgette soup

1 Heat the oil in a saucepan, add the garlic, tomatoes and tomato purée and cook over a gentle heat for 10 minutes. Stir in the basil and stock with salt and pepper to taste. Bring to the boil, lower the heat and simmer for 5 minutes.

2 Cool the soup slightly, then purée it in a food processor or liquidizer until fairly smooth. Leave to cool. Stir the courgettes into the soup; cover and chill for 4 hours, or overnight.

3 Just before serving, place an ice cube in each of 4 chilled soup bowls. Pour in the soup, add a swirl of yogurt and garnish with basil leaves.

3 tablespoons olive oil

1 garlic clove, crushed

1 kg (2 lb) tomatoes, skinned, deseeded and chopped

2 tablespoons tomato purée

1 tablespoon chopped basil

750 ml (1¼ pints) Chicken Stock (see page 8)

2 courgettes, trimmed and coarsely grated

salt and pepper

**To Garnish:**

4 ice cubes

3 tablespoons low-fat natural yogurt

basil leaves

---

**Serves 4**

---

**Preparation time:** about 15 minutes, plus cooling and chilling

---

**Cooking time:** about 20 minutes

---

**kcal** 132; **kJ** 552; **protein** 4 g; **fat** 9 g; **CHO** 9 g

■ Choose dark red, sun-ripened tomatoes, such as Italian plum tomatoes, for this soup. They will give it a deeper colour and more intense flavour than hothouse tomatoes.

1 Melt the butter or margarine in a saucepan, add the onion and cook over a moderate heat until soft but not golden, stirring frequently.

2 Add the peas, sugar, stock and 3 tablespoons of the chopped mint. Stir in white pepper to taste and bring the mixture to the boil. Add the potatoes, lower the heat and simmer, partially covered, for 20–25 minutes.

3 Cool the mixture slightly, then purée it in batches in a food processor or liquidizer until smooth. Return to a clean saucepan, season with salt, add the milk and stir well. Heat the soup gently without boiling. Serve in warmed soup plates or bowls, garnished with the remaining chopped mint.

25 g (1 oz) butter or margarine

1 small onion, chopped

500 g (1 lb) frozen green peas

¼ teaspoon sugar

1.2 litres (2 pints) Chicken or Vegetable Stock (see page 8)

4 tablespoons chopped mint

300 g (10 oz) potatoes, peeled and coarsely chopped

150 ml (¼ pint) semi-skimmed milk

salt and white pepper

| Serves 6 |
| --- |
| **Preparation time:** 5–10 minutes |
| **Cooking time:** 30–35 minutes |
| kcal 148; **kJ** 624; **protein** 7 g; **fat** 5 g; **CHO** 20 g |

# pea & mint soup

# honey carrots

1 Pour the water into a medium saucepan. Add the carrots and bring to the boil. Reduce the heat, cover and simmer for about 10 minutes, or until the carrots are tender-crisp, and drain. If using frozen carrots, follow the packet directions for cooking.

2 Melt the margarine in a frying pan over a medium-high heat. Add the sugar, honey and carrots. Reduce the heat and turn the carrots frequently for 1–2 minutes until well glazed. Sprinkle the parsley over the carrots before serving them.

125 ml (4 fl oz) water

750 g (1½ lb) baby carrots, fresh or frozen

1 tablespoon margarine

½ tablespoon soft light brown sugar

2 tablespoons clear honey

2–3 tablespoons finely chopped parsley

| Serves 6 |
| --- |
| **Preparation time:** 10 minutes |
| **Cooking time:** about 15 minutes |
| kcal 87; **kJ** 365; **protein** 1 g; **fat** 3 g; **CHO** 16 g |

# medley of spring vegetables

1 Blanch the broad beans, if using fresh, the mangetout or peas and asparagus separately in salted boiling water and refresh immediately in cold water. Drain and set aside. Pop the broad beans out of their skins.

2 Melt the butter or margarine in a large flameproof casserole over a low heat, add the spring onions and garlic and cook, without colouring, until softened. Add the stock and thyme, bring to the boil and add the baby onions, then cover and simmer for 5 minutes.

3 Add the turnips, bring back to the boil, reduce the heat and simmer for 6–8 minutes. Add the carrots and cook for 5–6 minutes. Season with salt, pepper and lemon juice. Add the beans, peas and asparagus and heat through. Serve at once, garnished with the chervil.

250 g (8 oz) small broad beans, defrosted if frozen

175 g (6 oz) mangetout or sugar snap peas, trimmed

175 g (6 oz) fine young asparagus, trimmed and cut into 2.5 cm (1 inch) pieces

25 g (1 oz) butter or margarine

8 spring onions, sliced

2 garlic cloves, chopped

900 ml (1½ pints) Chicken or Vegetable Stock (see page 8)

1 thyme sprig

15 baby onions, peeled

10 baby turnips or 3 small turnips, cut into wedges

250 g (8 oz) baby carrots

1½ tablespoons lemon juice

salt and pepper

chervil, to garnish

**Serves 4**

**Preparation time:** 20–25 minutes

**Cooking time:** 25 minutes

**kcal** 217; **kJ** 908; **protein** 11 g; **fat** 7 g; **CHO** 29 g

# bean sprout salad

1 Put the mushrooms into a large salad bowl and pour over the French dressing. Toss lightly and leave to stand for 30 minutes.

2 Add all the remaining ingredients to the salad bowl and toss well. Serve the salad at once.

125 g (4 oz) button mushrooms, thinly sliced

2 tablespoons French Dressing (see page 64)

500 g (1 lb) fresh bean sprouts

4 carrots, trimmed and cut into thin sticks

250 g (8 oz) red cabbage, thinly shredded

3 cartons cress

**Serves 4**

**Preparation time:** 20 minutes, plus standing

kcal 120; **kJ** 499; **protein** 5 g; **fat** 7 g; **CHO** 11 g

■ Canned bean sprouts are a handy storecupboard item. You could use two 410 g (13½ oz) cans, well drained, instead of the fresh bean sprouts used in this recipe.

low fat

2 courgettes, sliced

24 yellow or red cherry tomatoes, or a mixture of both

1 onion, cut into 8 wedges

8 shiitake mushrooms

**Marinade:**

1 tablespoon soy sauce

2 tablespoons olive oil

1 teaspoon wholegrain mustard

salt and pepper

# tomato & vegetable kebabs

| Serves 4 |
| --- |
| **Preparation time:** 10 minutes, plus marinating |
| **Cooking time:** 6–10 minutes |
| kcal 123; **kJ** 514; **protein** 4 g; **fat** 7 g; **CHO** 13 g |

1 Mix the marinade ingredients together in a bowl. Bring a saucepan of water to the boil. Add the courgette slices and blanch for 1 minute. Drain well.

2 Thread the cherry tomatoes, courgette slices, onion wedges and mushrooms on to 4 long or 8 short skewers and brush with the marinade. Leave the kebabs to marinate for 30 minutes.

3 Cook the kebabs under a preheated grill or on a barbecue for about 5–10 minutes, turning them from time to time, and serve at once. Plain boiled rice or a salad would make a good accompaniment to this dish.

■ You can vary the vegetables according to availability. Try adding artichoke hearts, new potatoes, baby leeks, peas, patty pan squash or baby courgettes. (This will of course change the nutritional information.)

# griddled asparagus

1 Heat the oil, if using, in the griddle pan and place the asparagus on it in a single layer. Cook for about 5 minutes, turning occasionally. The asparagus should be tender when pierced with the tip of a sharp knife, and lightly patched with brown. Remove the asparagus from the pan to a shallow dish, sprinkle it with sea salt and pepper and set aside.

2 To make the tarragon and lemon dressing, mix all the ingredients together in a screw-top jar and shake well to combine. Pour 4 tablespoons of the dressing over the asparagus and toss gently, then leave to cool and marinate for at least 5 minutes (the longer, the better).

3 Arrange the rocket on a platter, sprinkle the spring onions and radishes over the top and arrange the asparagus in a pile in the middle of the leaves. Garnish with herbs and thin strips of lemon rind. Serve the asparagus on its own with bread or as an accompaniment to a main dish.

3 tablespoons olive oil (optional)

500 g (1 lb) asparagus, trimmed

125 g (4 oz) rocket or other green leaves

2 spring onions, finely sliced

4 radishes, thinly sliced

sea salt flakes and pepper

**Tarragon and Lemon Dressing:**

2 tablespoons tarragon vinegar

finely grated rind of 1 lemon

¼ teaspoon Dijon mustard

pinch of sugar

1 tablespoon chopped tarragon

5 tablespoons olive oil or grapeseed oil

salt and pepper

**To Garnish:**

coarsely chopped herbs, such as tarragon, parsley, chervil and dill

thin strips of lemon rind

**Serves 4**

**Preparation time:** 15 minutes, plus marinating

**Cooking time:** about 5 minutes

kcal 106; **kJ** 437; **protein** 5 g; **fat** 8 g; **CHO** 5 g

# aubergine & red pepper layer toasts

1 Cut the aubergine into 5 mm (¼ inch) thick slices, brush with a little oil and place on a grill rack. Cook under a preheated grill for 2–3 minutes on each side until charred and tender. Remove and set aside to cool.

2 Grill the pepper quarters, skin-side up, until the skins are charred. Transfer to a plastic bag and leave to soften for 15 minutes.

3 Meanwhile, toast the bread on both sides and immediately rub it all over with the cut sides of garlic and then the cut sides of the tomato. Brush with any remaining oil.

4 Peel off and discard the charred pepper skins and cut the flesh into wide strips. Layer the aubergine and peppers over the toast. Cut the goats' cheese into 4 slices and place 1 slice on top of each piece of toast. Season with pepper. Return to the grill for 1–2 minutes until the cheese is bubbling and melted. Garnish with the parsley and serve at once.

1 small aubergine

1 tablespoon extra virgin olive oil

2 large red peppers, cored, deseeded and quartered

4 large slices day-old wholemeal bread

1 garlic clove, peeled and halved

1 ripe tomato, halved

125 g (4 oz) goats' cheese

pepper

flat leaf parsley, to garnish

**Serves 4**

**Preparation time:** 20 minutes

**Cooking time:** about 15 minutes

kcal 219; kJ 919; protein 10 g; fat 9 g; CHO 26 g

# warm salad of turkey, red pepper & lemon

1 Whisk the dressing ingredients in a bowl until thickened. Tear the lettuce leaves roughly and put them into a large salad bowl.

2 Heat the oil in a heavy-based pan and fry the red pepper strips in it, stirring frequently, for 5 minutes. Add the turkey strips and cook, stirring, for another 5 minutes until tender and heated through.

3 Remove the turkey and pepper strips from the pan with a slotted spoon and arrange on top of the lettuce.

4 Pour the dressing into the pan, increase the heat to high and stir until sizzling. Pour the dressing over the salad and toss. Serve at once, garnished with lemon wedges.

2 Little Gem lettuces, leaves separated

1 tablespoon extra virgin olive oil

1 red pepper, cored, deseeded and cut lengthways into thin strips

500 g (1 lb) cooked turkey, cut diagonally into thin strips

lemon wedges, to garnish

**Dressing:**

1½ tablespoons extra virgin olive oil

2 tablespoons lemon juice

1 garlic clove, crushed

1 teaspoon Dijon mustard

salt and pepper

**Serves 4**

**Preparation time:** 10 minutes

**Cooking time:** 10 minutes

kcal 243; **kJ** 1018; **protein** 38 g; **fat** 9 g; **CHO** 3 g

# smoked salmon pancakes

1 Pour 175 ml (6 fl oz) of the milk into a pan. Heat until the milk rises, then remove the pan from the heat and allow the milk to cool. If using fresh yeast, mix with the water; if using dried yeast, sprinkle it over the water. Leave for 5 minutes until frothy.

2 Sift the flours and salt into a bowl. Mix thoroughly, then make a well in the centre. Add the yeast mixture and the scalded milk, and gradually incorporate the flour. Beat for 2 minutes until smooth. Cover with a damp tea towel and put in a warm place for 2–3 hours to rise.

3 Melt half the butter in a pan and allow to cool a little. Add a further 50 ml (2 fl oz) of the milk to the risen batter, stirring it in thoroughly. Stir in the egg yolks, soured cream and melted butter until the mixture has the consistency of double cream. (If it is too thick to pour, add more milk.) Whisk the egg whites until stiff peaks form. Fold into the batter, a little at a time, until thoroughly mixed.

4 Heat half the remaining butter in a frying pan. Pour enough batter into the pan to make a small pancake about 10 cm (4 inches) wide. Cook for 1–2 minutes, turning when browned. Keep warm while making the remaining pancakes. Add more butter to the pan as necessary until all the batter is used. Serve hot with smoked salmon and crème fraîche, garnished with salmon eggs and dill sprigs.

250–300 ml (8–10 fl oz) skimmed milk

15 g (½ oz) fresh yeast or 15 g (½ oz) fast-action dried yeast

4 tablespoons water

50 g (2 oz) plain flour

100 g (3½ oz) buckwheat flour

½ teaspoon salt

50 g (2 oz) butter

2 eggs, separated

2 tablespoons soured cream

**To Serve:**

125 g (4 oz) smoked salmon

175 g (6 oz) half-fat crème fraîche

**To Garnish:**

salmon eggs

dill sprigs

---

**Makes 8**

**Preparation time:** 10 minutes, plus standing

**Cooking time:** about 20 minutes

**Each pancake:**
kcal 188; kJ 784; **protein** 9 g; **fat** 9 g; **CHO** 19 g

# seafood salad

1 Cut the bodies of the squid into rings about 5 mm (¼ inch) thick; leave the tentacles whole. Put the squid rings and tentacles into a shallow pan with 2 tablespoons of the lemon juice, the fish stock, parsley and salt and pepper to taste; cook gently in a covered pan for 10 minutes until the squid is just tender.

2 Meanwhile, scrub and debeard the mussels, discarding any with open or broken shells. Put the mussels into a pan with the garlic, dill, white wine and salt and pepper to taste. Cover and cook for 5 minutes, shaking the pan from time to time, until the shells open. Discard any mussels that have not opened.

3 Drain the cooked squid, discarding the cooking liquid. Remove the mussels from the pan with a slotted spoon, reserving their cooking liquid. Shell some of the mussels and leave the remainder in their shells. Remove the heads neatly from the Mediterranean prawns, leaving the body shells and tails intact. Mix the squid, shelled mussels, prawns and cockles together in a large bowl.

4 Mix the oil with the remaining lemon juice, 3 tablespoons of the strained mussel cooking liquid and salt and pepper to taste. Stir the dressing into the shellfish. Arrange a bed of samphire or spinach leaves on each of 4 plates and spoon the prepared seafood salad on top. Serve, garnished with the unshelled mussels and a few pieces of curly endive.

375 g (12 oz) fresh squid, skinned and cleaned

juice of 2 lemons

300 ml (½ pint) Fish Stock (see page 9)

2 tablespoons chopped parsley

500 g (l lb) fresh mussels

2 garlic cloves, finely chopped

1 tablespoon chopped dill

300 ml (½ pint) dry white wine

8 cooked Mediterranean prawns

125 g (4 oz) cooked cockles

2 tablespoons olive oil

salt and pepper

samphire or spinach leaves, to serve

curly endive, to garnish

| **Serves 4** |
| --- |
| **Preparation time:** 35 minutes |
| **Cooking time:** 15–20 minutes |
| kcal 237; kJ 993; protein 27 g; fat 8 g; CHO 3 g |

1 Bring a large saucepan of salted water to the boil. Add the pasta, stir and cook for 10–12 minutes until just tender. Rinse under cold running water and drain thoroughly.

2 Put the radishes and cucumber into a bowl and add the pasta. Stir in the yogurt and season with a little salt and plenty of pepper. Toss the pasta, radishes and cucumber in the yogurt to coat thoroughly.

3 Arrange the lettuce leaves on a serving dish and spoon the salad into them. Garnish with the chopped spring onions.

125 g (4 oz) dried pasta shapes

175 g (6 oz) radishes, sliced

½ cucumber, about 250 g (8 oz), unpeeled and diced

150 ml (¼ pint) low-fat natural yogurt

1 Cos lettuce

salt and pepper

2 finely chopped spring onions, to garnish

| Serves 4 |
| --- |
| **Preparation time:** 20 minutes |
| **Cooking time:** about 12 minutes |
| kcal 149; **kJ** 630; **protein** 7 g; **fat** 1 g; **CHO** 29 g |

# pasta, cucumber & radish salad

# pasta slaw

1 Bring a saucepan of lightly salted water to the boil. Add the pasta, stir and cook for 10–12 minutes until just tender. At the same time, bring a second pan of lightly salted water to the boil and cook the French beans for 3–5 minutes. Refresh the pasta and beans under cold running water, drain and leave to cool.

2 Meanwhile, mix together the remaining salad ingredients in a bowl. Combine the ingredients for the dressing in a jug and add to the salad bowl with the pasta and French beans. Season to taste with salt and pepper, garnish with parsley sprigs, if using, and serve.

75 g (3 oz) dried pasta spirals (fusilli)

300 g (10 oz) French beans

75 g (3 oz) white cabbage, roughly chopped

1 carrot, grated

4 spring onions, finely chopped

salt and pepper

parsley sprigs, to garnish (optional)

**Dressing:**

4 tablespoons low-fat mayonnaise

2 tablespoons skimmed milk

1 tablespoon balsamic or wine vinegar

2 teaspoons sugar

salt and pepper

| |
|---|
| **Makes 4** |
| **Preparation time:** 10 minutes, plus cooling |
| **Cooking time:** 10–12 minutes |
| kcal 146; **kJ** 612; **protein** 5 g; **fat** 5 g; **CHO** 22 g |

# coast to coast

# sweet & sour vegetables

1 Heat the oil in a wok or heavy-based, deep-sided frying pan, add the garlic and fry quickly. When the garlic is turning golden, add all the remaining ingredients except the spring onions, and cook, stirring constantly, for 2–3 minutes. Taste and adjust the seasoning, then add the chopped spring onions and cook for 30 seconds. Serve at once.

2 tablespoons groundnut oil

3 garlic cloves, chopped

1 cucumber, halved, deseeded and chopped diagonally into 5 mm (¼ inch) slices

4 baby sweetcorns, sliced diagonally

1 tomato, cut into 8 pieces

250 g (8 oz) can water chestnuts, drained

50 g (2 oz) mangetout, topped and tailed

1 onion, roughly chopped

4 tablespoons Vegetable Stock (see page 8)

1 tablespoon sugar

1 tablespoon fish sauce or soy sauce

1 tablespoon distilled white vinegar or Chinese rice vinegar

3 spring onions, roughly chopped

| Serves 4 |
| --- |
| **Preparation time:** 15 minutes |
| **Cooking time:** 5 minutes |
| kcal 133; **kJ** 554; **protein** 3 g; **fat** 6 g; **CHO** 18 g |

■ Fish sauce, a salty, thin brown liquid, is a basic of South-east Asian cooking. Called 'nam pla' in Thai cooking, it is available in oriental stores and larger supermarkets. If you cannot find it, soy sauce or anchovy essence make good substitutes.

# stir-fried summer vegetables

1 Heat the oil in a wok or deep frying pan, add the spring onions, ginger and garlic and stir-fry for about 30 seconds.

2 Add the chillies and all the vegetables. Toss well and cook, stirring, for 2 minutes. Stir in the soy sauce and sherry and cook for a further 2 minutes.

3 Sprinkle over the sesame oil, pile the vegetables into a warmed serving dish and serve immediately.

2 tablespoons vegetable oil

2 spring onions, sliced

2.5 cm (1 inch) piece of fresh root ginger, peeled and sliced

2 garlic cloves, sliced

2 chillies, deseeded and chopped

50 g (2 oz) button mushrooms

125 g (4 oz) baby carrots

125 g (4 oz) mangetout

125 g (4 oz) French beans

50 g (2 oz) bean sprouts

1 red pepper, cored, deseeded and sliced

2 celery sticks, sliced

few cauliflower florets

4 tablespoons light soy sauce

2 tablespoons dry sherry

1 teaspoon sesame oil

**Serves 4**

**Preparation time:** 10 minutes

**Cooking time:** 5 minutes

kcal 125; **kJ** 520; **protein** 5 g; **fat** 7 g; **CHO** 9 g

# caponata

1 Heat the oil in a heavy-based saucepan, add the onion and fry gently until soft and golden. Add the celery and cook for 2–3 minutes. Add the aubergine and cook gently for 3 minutes, stirring occasionally.

2 Add the passata and cook gently until it has been absorbed. Add the wine vinegar and cook for 1 minute. Add the peppers, anchovies, capers and olives and cook for a further 3 minutes. Season to taste with salt.

3 Transfer the mixture to an ovenproof dish, cover and bake in a preheated oven, 180°C (350°F), Gas Mark 4, for about 1 hour. Serve the caponata lukewarm or cold, sprinkled with chopped parsley.

2 tablespoons olive oil

1 onion, thinly sliced

2 celery sticks, diced

3 aubergines, trimmed and cut into 1 cm (½ inch) dice

150 ml (¼ pint) passata

3 tablespoons wine vinegar

1 yellow pepper, cored, deseeded and thinly sliced

1 red pepper, cored, deseeded and thinly sliced

25 g (1 oz) anchovy fillets, soaked in warm water, drained and dried

50 g (2 oz ) capers, roughly chopped

25 g (1 oz) black olives, pitted and sliced

25 g (1 oz) green olives, pitted and sliced

salt

2 tablespoons chopped parsley, to garnish

**Serves 6**

**Preparation time:** 40 minutes

**Cooking time:** about 1 hour

kcal 74; **kJ** 313; **protein** 3 g; **fat** 4 g; **CHO** 7 g

# chickpea & red pepper salad

1 Cook the chickpeas in unsalted boiling water for 1–2 hours, or until they are tender. Meanwhile, place the red peppers under a hot grill for 15 minutes, turning them frequently, until the skins blacken and blister. Hold the peppers under cold water then, using a small sharp knife, peel off the skins. Halve the peppers, remove the cores and seeds and slice the flesh.

2 Mix the dressing ingredients together. Drain the chickpeas and toss in the dressing while they are still hot. Set aside to cool. Stir in the peppers, olives and half the coriander. Turn the salad into a serving dish and serve, sprinkled with the remaining coriander and the orange rind.

175 g (6 oz) dried chickpeas, soaked overnight and drained

3 red peppers

12 black olives, pitted

2 tablespoons chopped fresh coriander

thin strips of orange rind, to garnish

**Dressing:**

2 tablespoons sunflower oil

½ teaspoon grated orange rind

2 tablespoons orange juice

1 garlic clove, crushed

salt and pepper

| Serves 4 |
| --- |
| **Preparation time:** 10 minutes, plus soaking |
| **Cooking time:** 1–2 hours |
| kcal 227; **kJ** 955; **protein** 11 g; **fat** 9 g; **CHO** 28 g |

■ Chickpeas vary in their cooking time – the older they are the longer they take, so taste them frequently as they cook.

4 artichokes, stems trimmed and top third of leaves removed

1 tablespoon lemon juice

3 carrots, cut into 5 mm (¼ inch) rounds

75 g (3 oz) cauliflower florets

75 g (3 oz) broccoli florets

2 small courgettes, cut into 1 cm (½ inch) rounds

4 tablespoons tomato purée

3.5 cm (1½ inch) piece of fresh root ginger, peeled and cut into thin strips

## Sauce:

150 g (5 oz) tofu, drained

4 tablespoons tomato purée

4 tablespoons horseradish sauce

2 teaspoons lemon juice

2 teaspoons white vinegar

½ teaspoon Lemon Herb Seasoning (see page 9)

½ teaspoon onion salt

½ teaspoon sugar

few drops Tabasco sauce

freshly ground white pepper

1 Place the artichokes and lemon juice in a deep saucepan and add boiling water to cover. Cover and cook for 30 minutes, or until one of the artichoke leaves pulls off easily. Remove the artichokes from the pan, turn them upside down to drain, then refrigerate to cool.

2 Meanwhile, place all the vegetables in a medium saucepan with the tomato purée and ginger. Steam for 7 minutes until tender, then refrigerate to cool. Once the artichokes and vegetables are chilled, remove the central choke of each artichoke and fill with the vegetables.

3 To make the sauce, place all the ingredients in a blender or food processor and purée. Pour some sauce over each artichoke to serve.

### Serves 8

**Preparation time:** 30 minutes, plus chilling

**Cooking time:** about 35 minutes

kcal 133; kJ 558; protein 9 g; fat 3 g; CHO 17 g

# chilled stuffed artichokes

# prawn creole

1 Place the onion, green pepper, tomatoes and their juice, basil, oregano and sugar in a heavy-based saucepan. Add salt and pepper to taste. Bring to the boil, cover and simmer for 15 minutes. Add the turbot and peeled prawns and simmer for a further 10–15 minutes.

2 Mix the cornflour and wine together until smooth, then stir into the pan. Heat gently, stirring, until the sauce thickens and continue cooking for 2 minutes. Transfer to a warmed serving dish and serve garnished with the Mediterranean prawns and chopped parsley.

1 onion, chopped

1 green pepper, cored, deseeded and chopped

400 g (13 oz) can chopped tomatoes

½ teaspoon dried basil

½ teaspoon dried oregano

pinch of sugar

250 g (8 oz) turbot (or other white fish) fillets, cut into cubes

250 g (8 oz) peeled raw prawns

2 teaspoons cornflour

2 tablespoons dry white wine

salt and pepper

**To Garnish:**

whole cooked Mediterranean prawns

chopped parsley

| Serves 4 |
| --- |
| **Preparation time:** 15 minutes |
| **Cooking time:** 30–35 minutes |
| kcal 182; **kJ** 770; **protein** 27 g; **fat** 3 g; **CHO** 11 g |

500 g (1 lb) fresh spinach, cooked and chopped

freshly ground nutmeg

3 tablespoons fromage frais

1 garlic clove, crushed

125 g (4 oz) cooked, peeled prawns

125 g (4 oz) shelled, cooked mussels

1 egg yolk

250 g (8 oz) fresh green lasagne

125 g (4 oz) low-fat soft cheese

150 ml (¼ pint) low-fat natural yogurt

1 egg, beaten

2 tablespoons grated Parmesan cheese

salt and pepper

tarragon sprigs, to garnish

| Serves 6 |
| --- |
| **Preparation time:** 10 minutes |
| **Cooking time:** 35–40 minutes |
| kcal 192; **kJ** 805; **protein** 18 g; **fat** 9 g; **CHO** 11 g |

1 Mix the spinach with the nutmeg and salt and pepper to taste. Stir in the fromage frais, garlic, prawns, mussels and egg yolk.

2 Place half the spinach mixture in a lightly greased deep ovenproof dish and top with half the lasagne; add the soft cheese in small knobs, top with the remaining spinach mixture and then the rest of the lasagne.

3 To make the sauce, mix the yogurt with the egg and spoon over the top layer of lasagne. Sprinkle with the grated Parmesan cheese.

4 Transfer to a preheated oven, 190°C (375°F), Gas Mark 5, and bake for 35–40 minutes, until bubbling and golden. Serve piping hot, cut into wedges, and garnished with tarragon. A mixed salad makes a good accompaniment.

# seafood lasagne

# stir-fried garlic lamb

1 Cut the lamb into thin slices across the grain. Mix the sherry with the soy sauces and sesame oil in a shallow dish. Add the lamb and toss it in the mixture to coat. Leave to marinate for 15 minutes then drain, reserving the marinade.

2 Heat the oil in a wok or deep-sided frying pan, add the meat and about 2 teaspoons of the marinade and stir-fry briskly for about 2 minutes, until well browned. Add the garlic, ginger, leek and spring onions and stir-fry for a further 3 minutes. Serve at once, garnished with a spring onion fan.

300 g (10 oz) lamb fillet

2 tablespoons dry sherry

2 tablespoons light soy sauce

1 tablespoon dark soy sauce

1 teaspoon sesame oil

2 teaspoons vegetable oil

6 garlic cloves, thinly sliced

2.5 cm (1 inch) piece of fresh root ginger, peeled and chopped

1 leek, thinly sliced diagonally

4 spring onions, chopped

spring onion fan, to garnish

**Serves 4**

**Preparation time:** 20 minutes, plus marinating

**Cooking time:** 5 minutes

kcal 162; kJ 679; protein 17 g; fat 9 g; CHO 2 g

# sweet & sour turkey

1 tablespoon vegetable oil

1 onion, finely chopped

1 boneless turkey breast, skinned and cubed

½ yellow or red pepper, cored, deseeded and sliced

3 mushrooms, sliced

spring onion fan, to garnish

**Sauce:**

1½ tablespoons soy sauce

1 tablespoon tomato purée

2 teaspoons cornflour

300 ml (½ pint) water

3 tablespoons unsweetened pineapple juice

2 tablespoons wine vinegar

1 teaspoon brown sugar

1 To make the sauce, place all the ingredients in a small pan and mix well. Bring to the boil, then simmer, stirring until thickened. Keep warm.

2 Heat the oil in a wok, or deep-sided frying pan, add the onion and stir-fry for 2 minutes. Add the turkey and stir-fry for 2–3 minutes. Add the pepper and mushrooms and cook for a further 2–3 minutes.

3 Transfer to a warmed serving dish and pour over the sauce. Serve garnished with the spring onion fan.

| Serves 4 |
| --- |
| **Preparation time:** 6 minutes |
| **Cooking time:** about 10 minutes |
| kcal 230; kJ 972; **protein** 36 g; **fat** 5 g; **CHO** 12 g |

■ Serve this speedy stir-fry recipe with boiled rice and a green vegetable such as French beans or mangetout.

1 Combine the ginger, garlic, soy sauce, sherry, chilli sauce, honey and five-spice powder in a bowl. Stir well. Add the steak, stir to coat thoroughly, then cover and leave to marinate for at least 30 minutes.

2 Bring a large saucepan of lightly salted water to the boil. Add the noodles, remove the pan from the heat, cover and leave to stand for 5 minutes.

3 Meanwhile, heat a wok or frying pan. Add 2 tablespoons of the marinade and the beef and stir-fry for about 3–6 minutes. Then add the mangetout and remaining marinade to the wok, with salt and pepper if required, and stir-fry for a further 2 minutes.

4 Drain the noodles and arrange them in warmed serving bowls. Spoon the beef and mangetout over the top, garnish with shredded spring onions and serve.

25 g (1 oz) fresh root ginger, shredded

1 garlic clove, crushed

4 tablespoons light soy sauce

2 tablespoons dry sherry

1 teaspoon chilli sauce

1 teaspoon clear honey

½ teaspoon Chinese five-spice powder

375 g (12 oz) fillet steak, finely sliced

250 g (8 oz) dried egg noodles

250 g (8 oz) mangetout, trimmed

salt and pepper

shredded spring onions, to garnish

| Serves 4 |
| --- |
| **Preparation time:** 10 minutes, plus marinating and standing |
| **Cooking time:** 5–8 minutes |
| kcal 348; **kJ** 1475; **protein** 27 g; **fat** 5 g; **CHO** 50 g |

# beef & mangetout stir-fry

# pepper chicken

1 Mix the water with the hot chilli sauce and soy sauce in a jug or bowl. Set aside.

2 Heat the oil in a wok or deep-sided frying pan over a moderate heat. Add the spring onions, ginger and garlic and stir-fry for 30 seconds. Add the chicken strips, increase the heat to high and stir-fry for 3–4 minutes or until lightly coloured on all sides.

3 Add the chilli sauce mixture and toss until all the ingredients are well combined and piping hot. Serve at once, garnished with spring onions, if liked.

4 tablespoons water

2 tablespoons hot chilli sauce, or to taste

1 tablespoon soy sauce

2 tablespoons vegetable oil

2–4 spring onions, thinly sliced diagonally

5 cm (2 inch) piece of fresh root ginger, peeled and finely chopped

1 garlic clove, crushed

4 boneless, skinless chicken breasts, cut into thin strips across the grain

spring onions, to garnish (optional)

| Serves 4 |
| --- |
| **Preparation time:** 20 minutes |
| **Cooking time:** about 5 minutes |
| kcal 194; **kJ** 814; **protein** 27 g; **fat** 9 g; **CHO** 1 g |

# chicken tikka

1 Put the chicken in a large bowl and add the lemon juice, working it in with the fingers, to 'de-grease' the chicken in preparation for the marinade. Leave to stand for 1 hour, then strain off and discard the juices.

2 Mix together all the ingredients for the tandoori marinade and pour over the chicken. Cover and refrigerate for a minimum of 6 hours or overnight, but preferably for 24 hours.

3 Thread the tikkas on to metal skewers and place over barbecue coals for 10–15 minutes, turning them 2 or 3 times. Alternatively, the tikkas can be grilled, baked in a preheated oven, 190°C (375°F), Gas Mark 5, or even stir-fried (without oil) for about 15 minutes in each case. Serve with a salad.

500 g (1 lb) boneless, skinless chicken breast, diced

6–8 tablespoons lemon juice

**Tandoori Marinade:**

75 ml (3 fl oz) low-fat natural yogurt

75 ml (3 fl oz) semi-skimmed milk

1 tablespoon mild curry powder

2 teaspoons garam masala

1–4 teaspoons chilli powder (optional)

1 teaspoon paprika

1 tablespoon chopped mint

1½ tablespoons chopped coriander

1 tablespoon garlic purée

2.5 cm (1 inch) piece of fresh root ginger, peeled and chopped

2 teaspoons white cumin seeds, roasted and ground

2 tablespoons lemon juice

salad, to serve

**Serves 4** as a starter

**Preparation time:** 25 minutes, plus standing and marinating

**Cooking time:** 10–15 minutes

**kcal** 182; **kJ** 769; **protein** 30 g; **fat** 5 g; **CHO** 5 g

# chicken fajitas

1 To make the marinde, combine all the ingredients in a bowl. Add the chicken, toss to coat evenly and leave in the refrigerator for 10–20 minutes, turning at least once.

2 Heat the oil in a frying pan over a medium-high heat. Add the onion and green pepper and fry, stirring constantly, for about 5 minutes, or until the onion is slightly brown. Remove the onion and pepper from the pan and keep warm.

3 Wrap the tortillas in foil and place on the lower shelf of a preheated oven, 200°C (400°F), Gas Mark 6. Then line a grill pan with foil, place the chicken strips on the foil and cook under a preheated grill about 7 cm (3 inches) from the heat for 4 minutes, turning once.

4 Place 3 chicken strips on each tortilla and top with the onions, green peppers and assorted garnishes as desired. Roll the tortilla around the chicken strips and serve, garnished with lemon wedges.

625 g (1¼ lb) boneless, skinless chicken breasts, cut into thin strips

2 teaspoons vegetable oil

1 large onion, cut into thin strips

1 large green pepper, cored, deseeded and cut into thin strips

8 flour tortillas

lemon wedges, to garnish

## Marinade:

1 garlic clove, finely chopped

1 tablespoon vegetable oil

1½ tablespoons lemon or lime juice

3 tablespoons Worcestershire sauce

¼ teaspoon pepper, or to taste

| Serves 6 |
| --- |
| **Preparation time:** 15 minutes, plus marinating |
| **Cooking time:** about 15 minutes |
| kcal 300; **kJ** 1270; **protein** 29 g; **fat** 5 g; **CHO** 34 g |

# chinese-style vermicelli

1 Bring a large saucepan of lightly salted water to the boil. Add the vermicelli, stir and bring back to the boil. Reduce the heat slightly and boil, uncovered, for 8–10 minutes, or until just tender, stirring occasionally.

2 Meanwhile, put the carrots, courgettes and mangetout into a colander or sieve and sprinkle with salt. Place the colander over a pan of boiling water. Cover the colander and steam the vegetables for about 5 minutes until they are tender but still crunchy. Remove the colander and set it aside. Drain the vermicelli while it is still just tender, and cut it into shorter lengths with kitchen scissors.

3 Heat the oil in a wok or deep-sided frying pan. Add the spring onions and ginger and cook gently, stirring, until the ingredients give off a spicy aroma. Add the remaining ingredients and stir well. Add the vermicelli and vegetables, then increase the heat and vigorously toss the ingredients until they are well combined and very hot. Season with pepper to taste. Turn into a warmed serving bowl and garnish with parsley leaves. Serve at once.

250 g (8 oz) dried vermicelli

4 carrots, cut into fine matchsticks

4 courgettes, cut into fine matchsticks

125 g (4 oz) small mangetout

5 teaspoons vegetable oil

4 spring onions, sliced diagonally

2.5 cm (1 inch) piece of fresh root ginger, peeled and sliced into matchsticks

1–2 garlic cloves, crushed

4 tablespoons light soy sauce

1 tablespoon clear honey

1 tablespoon white wine vinegar

1 teaspoon coriander seeds, crushed

salt and pepper

parsley leaves, to garnish

**Serves 4**

**Preparation time:** 15–20 minutes

**Cooking time:** about 15 minutes

**kcal** 320; **kJ** 1336; **protein** 9 g; **fat** 5 g; **CHO** 61 g

# spaghetti with anchovies

1 Bring a large saucepan of lightly salted water to the boil. Add the spaghetti, stir and cook for 10–12 minutes until just tender.

2 Meanwhile, chop the anchovies and put them in a medium saucepan with the garlic. Stir with a wooden spoon, pressing the anchovies so that they break up and become almost puréed. Add the orange rind and juice, the sugar and pepper to taste. Stir the sauce vigorously over a low heat until heated through and combined with the anchovies.

3 Drain the spaghetti well and turn it into a warmed serving bowl. Pour over the sauce, add the Parmesan and half the mint and toss together quickly. Serve at once, sprinkled with the remaining mint.

500 g (1 lb) dried spaghetti

2 x 50 g (2 oz) cans anchovies in oil, drained

1 garlic clove, crushed

finely grated rind and juice of 1 orange

pinch of sugar

½ tablespoon freshly grated Parmesan cheese

2 tablespoons chopped mint

salt and pepper

---

**Serves 6**

**Preparation time:** 15 minutes

**Cooking time:** about 15 minutes

kcal 345; **kJ** 1463; **protein** 15 g; **fat** 5 g; **CHO** 64 g

1 large onion, sliced

2 garlic cloves, crushed

500 g (1 lb) courgettes, chopped

1 green pepper, cored, deseeded and chopped

400 g (13 oz) can tomatoes, roughly chopped, with juice reserved

125 g (4 oz) black olives, pitted

3 anchovy fillets, finely chopped

1 tablespoon chopped parsley

2 teaspoons chopped marjoram

500 g (1 lb) dried pasta, such as tagliatelle

salt and pepper

few flat leaf parsley sprigs, to garnish

1 Heat a large, deep-sided frying pan or wok and dry-fry the onion and garlic for 3–6 minutes, stirring constantly, until soft. Add the courgettes with a little water and cook for 10 minutes. Add the green pepper, the tomatoes with their juice, olives, anchovies, parsley, marjoram and salt and pepper to taste. Bring to the boil, stirring. Cover the pan and simmer while cooking the pasta.

2 Meanwhile, bring a large saucepan of lightly salted water to the boil. Add the pasta, stir and cook for 10–12 minutes until just tender. Drain well and turn it into a warmed serving dish. Add the sauce and toss lightly together. Garnish with the parsley and serve at once.

| **Serves 6** |
| **Preparation time:** 15 minutes |
| **Cooking time:** about 30 minutes |
| kcal 345; **kJ** 1464; **protein** 13 g; **fat** 4 g; **CHO** 69 g |

# pasta syracuse style

trout in a paper bag ●

baked red mullet with limes ●

griddled tuna with ginger & rice noodles ●

monkfish kebabs with cumin & mint ●

haddock & spinach layer ●

thin steak on a bed of hot leaves ●

sirloin steaks with tomato-garlic sauce ●

roast pork fillet with rosemary & fennel ●

chicken véronique ●

turkey & ham kebabs ●

glazed turkey breasts with cranberry & ●
chestnut stuffing

tabbouleh & fennel salad ●

spaghetti with three herb sauce ●

pasta with spring vegetables ●

# main event

# trout in a paper bag

1 Cut 8 rectangles of greaseproof paper or kitchen foil double the width of each trout, and half as long again as the fish.

2 Place 4 of the rectangles on a baking sheet. Lay a trout along the centre of each one, pull up the edges of the paper or foil and fold at each corner so that the paper forms a container for each fish.

3 Sprinkle a little salt and pepper, garlic and herbs over each trout, then spoon 2 tablespoons of the wine over each one. Cover loosely with the remaining paper or foil and fold at the corners as before to form a lid over each fish. Fold the top and bottom layers of the paper or foil together in several places. Bake the trout in a preheated oven, 190°C (375°F), Gas Mark 5, for 35–40 minutes, until the fish is cooked. Take the fish to the table in the parcels, to serve.

4 small trout, about 125 g (4 oz) each, cleaned

2 garlic cloves, finely chopped

1 tablespoon chopped thyme

1 tablespoon chopped rosemary

150 ml (¼ pint) rosé wine

salt and pepper

| Serves 4 |
| --- |
| **Preparation time:** 30–35 minutes |
| **Cooking time:** 35–40 minutes |
| kcal 160; **kJ** 680; **protein** 23 g; **fat** 5 g; **CHO** 1 g |

# baked red mullet with limes

1 Make 2 or 3 cuts in the thickest part of each red mullet. Mix the lime rind with the green peppercorns and salt to taste. Press a little of this mixture inside each mullet, together with a sprig of thyme.

2 Lay the mullet in a lightly greased ovenproof dish, sprinkle with the lime juice, garlic and olive oil, and cover the dish. Transfer to a preheated oven, 190°C (375°F), Gas Mark 5, and cook for 15 minutes; remove the cover and continue baking for a further 10 minutes.

3 Serve the mullet garnished with wedges of lime and thyme sprigs.

4 red mullet, about 175 g (6 oz) each, gutted and cleaned

finely grated rind and juice of 2 limes

1 teaspoon green peppercorns

4 thyme sprigs, plus extra to garnish

2 garlic cloves, finely chopped

2 tablespoons olive oil

salt

thin wedges of lime, to garnish

| Serves 4 |
| --- |
| **Preparation time:** 20 minutes |
| **Cooking time:** 25 minutes |
| **kcal** 156; **kJ** 652; **protein** 22 g; **fat** 7 g; **CHO** 0 g |

■ Limes will grate more easily if they are cold, and if you use the coarse side of the grater.

# griddled tuna with ginger & rice noodles

1 Heat the grapeseed oil in a small saucepan and add the ginger, garlic, shallots, chilli and lemon grass. Heat gently, but do not allow to brown. Bring a large pan of water to the boil for the rice noodles.

2 Heat a heavy-based shallow frying pan or griddle and put the tuna fillet in it. Cook for 1–2 minutes on each side over a medium to high heat, gradually turning the fish so that it is charred all over. When cooked, remove the tuna from the pan or griddle and set aside to rest for 3 minutes.

3 Plunge the noodles into the boiling water and cook for 2 minutes, or according to the packet instructions. Drain well and return to the pan. Add the cooked ginger mixture, the lime rind and juice, soy sauce and sesame oil. Toss well, then cover and keep warm.

4 Cook the lime wedges in the frying pan or griddle on each side for 1 minute. This gives them a lovely charred effect and warms the juice slightly. Add the chopped coriander to the rice noodles and toss well. Arrange the noodles in a large serving dish. Cut the tuna into 1 cm (½ inch) slices and arrange on top of the rice noodles. Garnish with spring onion curls, the lime wedges and coriander, and serve immediately.

1 tablespoon grapeseed oil

5 cm (2 inch) piece of fresh root ginger, peeled and finely diced

2 garlic cloves, chopped

2 shallots, finely chopped

1 green chilli, deseeded and finely chopped

1 stalk lemon grass, finely sliced

400 g (13 oz) tuna fillet

250 g (8 oz) rice noodles

grated rind and juice of 1 lime

2 tablespoons soy sauce

2 teaspoons sesame oil

bunch of coriander, chopped

**To Garnish:**

spring onion curls

1 lime, cut into 4 wedges

coriander sprigs

| Serves 4 |
| --- |
| **Preparation time:** 15 minutes, plus resting |
| **Cooking time:** 10–15 minutes |

kcal 410; **kJ** 1719; **protein** 28 g; **fat** 9 g; **CHO** 53 g

■ Fresh tuna is is usually served pink and rare, but if this is not to your liking, just cook it a little longer.

1.5 kg (3 lb) monkfish, skinned and filleted

4 tablespoons olive oil

1 tablespoon lemon juice

1 tablespoon cumin seeds, lightly crushed

2 tablespoons finely chopped mint

salt and pepper

**Dip:**

150 ml (¼ pint) plain low-fat yogurt, chilled

1 cucumber, sliced and chopped

mint sprigs, to garnish

1 Cut the monkfish into bite-sized cubes and put them into a large, shallow dish. Combine the oil, lemon juice, cumin seeds and mint, season with salt and lots of black pepper, then pour over the fish, cover and leave to marinate for at least 1 hour.

2 Thread the fish on to 6 skewers and grill over a very hot barbecue or under a preheated hot grill for 4–5 minutes, turning every minute and brushing frequently with the marinade, until just cooked.

3 To make the dip, mix together the yogurt and chopped cucumber, and garnish with mint. Serve the kebabs immediately, with the dip, pitta bread and lettuce.

| Serves 6 |
| --- |
| **Preparation time:** 10 minutes, plus marinating |
| **Cooking time:** 4–5 minutes |
| kcal 218; **kJ** 918; **protein** 33 g; **fat** 9 g; **CHO** 3 g |

■ This dish may be prepared up to 24 hours in advance and kept chilled. Bring it to room temperature before cooking.

# monkfish kebabs with cumin & mint

500 g (1 lb) haddock fillets

150 ml (¼ pint) skimmed milk

1 bay leaf

1 hard-boiled egg, chopped

500 g (1 lb) frozen leaf spinach

salt and pepper

**Sauce:**

about 150 ml (¼ pint) skimmed milk

25 g (1 oz) margarine

1 onion, chopped

25 g (1 oz) plain flour

grated nutmeg

**Topping:**

2 crispbreads, crushed

1 tomato, sliced, to garnish

| Serves 4 |
| --- |
| **Preparation time:** 10 minutes |
| **Cooking time:** 35–45 minutes |
| kcal 266; **kJ** 1116; **protein** 30 g; **fat** 9 g; **CHO** 18 g |

1 Place the haddock in a pan. Add the milk, bay leaf and salt and pepper to taste, then poach for about 10 minutes until the fish is tender. Drain, reserving the liquor. Flake the haddock and mix with the egg. Cook the spinach as directed on the packet and drain well.

2 To make the sauce, pour the fish liquor into a measuring jug and make up to 300 ml (½ pint) with the milk. Melt the margarine in a pan and fry the onion until soft. Stir in the flour and cook for 1 minute. Gradually blend in the fish liquor and bring to the boil, stirring continuously. Cook, stirring, for a further 1 minute. Season to taste with salt, pepper and nutmeg. Stir in the fish and egg mixture and mix well.

3 Layer the spinach and fish mixture in a greased 1.2 litre (2 pint) ovenproof dish, finishing with a layer of spinach. Sprinkle with the crispbreads. Transfer the dish to a preheated oven, 180°C (350°F), Gas Mark 4, and cook for 20–30 minutes. Garnish with the tomato slices before serving.

# haddock & spinach layer

# thin steak on a bed of hot leaves

1 Using a rolling pin or meat mallet, gently beat each steak between layers of clingfilm until it is at least twice its original size.

2 To make the dressing, mix together the olive oil, lemon juice, red wine vinegar, mustard, sugar and salt and pepper. Pour over the hot salad leaves and toss well. Divide the salad leaves between 4 large plates.

3 Heat a griddle or shallow frying pan until very hot. Season the steaks on both sides, place on the pan and flash-cook on both sides, just long enough to sear the meat. Place on the salad leaves and serve immediately.

4 entrecôte steaks, about 125 g (4 oz) each, trimmed

250 g (8 oz) mixed hot salad leaves

**French Dressing:**

1 tablespoon olive oil

juice of 1 lemon

2 tablespoons red wine vinegar

½ teaspoon mustard

¼ teaspoon sugar

salt and pepper

| Serves 4 |
| --- |
| **Preparation time:** 15 minutes |
| **Cooking time:** about 6 minutes |
| kcal 205; **kJ** 857; **protein** 29 g; **fat** 9 g; **CHO** 1 g |

# sirloin steaks with tomato-garlic sauce

1 Beat the steaks with a meat mallet or rolling pin until fairly thin, then spread with the low-fat spread. Place the steaks on a grill rack and cook under a preheated hot grill for 8–10 minutes, or until cooked to your liking, turning them once.

2 Meanwhile, make the sauce. Place the tomatoes, garlic, basil and salt and pepper in a saucepan and simmer gently for about 10 minutes, until the tomatoes are soft.

3 Transfer the steaks to a warmed serving dish and pour over the sauce. Serve immediately, garnished with the basil. Serve with French beans, if liked.

4 sirloin steaks, about 50 g (2 oz) each, trimmed

2 teaspoons low-fat spread

basil sprigs, to garnish

French beans, to serve (optional)

**Tomato-garlic Sauce:**

750 g (1½ lb) tomatoes, skinned and chopped

3 garlic cloves, crushed

1 tablespoon chopped basil

salt and pepper

| |
|---|
| **Serves 4** |
| **Preparation time:** 10 minutes |
| **Cooking time:** about 20 minutes |
| kcal 140; **kJ** 590; **protein** 15 g; **fat** 5 g; **CHO** 6 g |

# roast pork fillet with rosemary & fennel

1 Break the rosemary into short pieces and slice the garlic coarsely. Heat 1 teaspoon of the olive oil in a nonstick frying pan, add the rosemary and garlic and fry gently for 1–2 minutes. Add the pork fillet and fry, turning it, for 5 minutes, or until it is browned all over. Remove the pork from the frying pan (don't clean the pan, although you may wish to remove the bits of rosemary and garlic with a slotted spoon).

2 Put the fennel in a nonstick roasting tin and drizzle with the remaining olive oil. Place the pork fillet on top and season it generously with salt and pepper. Transfer to a preheated oven, 230°C (450°F), Gas Mark 8, and roast for 20 minutes.

3 Meanwhile, pour the wine into the frying pan and simmer until it has reduced by half, scraping up any bits of pork fillet into the wine. Add the quark and season with salt and pepper. Stir well to mix.

4 To serve, cut the pork into slices and arrange on a warmed serving dish with the fennel. Pour the sauce into the roasting tin and cook over a moderate heat, using a wooden spoon to stir all the bits into the sauce. Spoon the heated sauce over the pork and fennel, garnish with rosemary sprigs and serve at once.

1 large rosemary sprig

3 garlic cloves

2 teaspoons olive oil

400 g (13 oz) pork fillet, trimmed

2 fennel bulbs, trimmed and cut into wedges, central core removed

150 ml (¼ pint) white wine

75 g (3 oz) quark

salt and pepper

rosemary sprigs, to garnish

| Serves 4 |
| --- |
| **Preparation time:** 10 minutes |
| **Cooking time:** about 30 minutes |
| kcal 206; **kJ** 860; **protein** 24 g; **fat** 9 g; **CHO** 2 g |

# 68

# chicken véronique

1 Trim any visible fat from the chicken breasts. Place the chicken breasts in a heavy-based frying pan, pour over the stock and bring to the boil. Cover the pan and simmer gently for 20 minutes, or until the chicken breasts are thoroughly cooked.

2 Remove the chicken breasts from the pan with a slotted spoon and keep warm. Strain the stock through a fine sieve into a measuring jug. Wipe the frying pan clean with kitchen paper and return 150 ml (¼ pint) of the stock to the clean pan.

3 Blend the cornflour to a smooth paste with a little of the milk, then add to the stock in the pan with the remaining milk. Bring to the boil over a moderate heat, stirring constantly. When the sauce has thickened, return the chicken breasts to the pan, add the halved grapes and simmer for 5 minutes until the chicken and grapes are heated through. Season to taste, then serve immediately with new potatoes and carrots, if liked.

4 boneless, skinless chicken breasts, about 150 g (5 oz) each

300 ml (½ pint) Chicken Stock (see page 8)

15 g (½ oz) cornflour

175 ml (6 fl oz) skimmed milk

200 g (7 oz) seedless green grapes, halved

salt and pepper

| Serves 4 |
| --- |
| **Preparation time:** 20 minutes |
| **Cooking time:** 30 minutes |
| **kcal** 230; **kJ** 966; **protein** 35 g; **fat** 5 g; **CHO** 13 g |

# turkey & ham kebabs

1 Put the turkey cubes into a shallow dish. Mix the lemon rind with the onion, garlic, pesto, basil and garlic oil, and salt and pepper to taste. Pour the mixture over the turkey, turning the pieces so that they are well coated. Cover the dish and chill in the refrigerator for 3–4 hours.

2 Drain the turkey, reserving the marinade. Wrap each piece of turkey in a strip of Parma ham. Thread the turkey and ham rolls on to kebab skewers, alternating them with the mushrooms, bay leaves and wedges of lemon.

3 Brush the threaded skewers with the reserved marinade. Put under a preheated grill and grill for 4–5 minutes. Turn the kebab skewers, brush once again with the marinade, and grill for a further 4–5 minutes. Serve the kebabs piping hot on a bed of shredded lettuce.

500 g (1 lb) turkey fillet, cut into 4 cm (1½ inch) cubes

grated rind of 1 lemon

1 small onion, finely chopped

1 garlic clove, finely chopped

1 teaspoon pesto

1 tablespoon basil and garlic oil (see Cook's Tip)

75 g (3 oz) Parma ham, cut into long strips

8 small button mushrooms

8 small bay leaves

8 lemon wedges

salt and pepper

shredded lettuce, to serve

**Serves 4**

**Preparation time:** 20 minutes, plus marinating

**Cooking time:** about 10 minutes

kcal 187; **kJ** 788; **protein** 33 g; **fat** 5 g; **CHO** 2 g

■ To make your own basil and garlic oil, steep 4 bruised garlic cloves, 2 tablespoons chopped basil and 1 teaspoon peppercorns in 600 ml (1 pint) olive oil for 1 week, shaking the bottle from time to time.

# 70

# glazed turkey breasts with cranberry & chestnut stuffing

1 To make the stuffing, lightly fry the onion in the oil until golden brown. Stir in the minced meat and breadcrumbs and cook for 2–3 minutes. Add the chestnuts, dried cranberries, thyme and sage. Mix well and season to taste. Remove from the heat and stir in the beaten egg. Spoon into a lightly greased 500 g (1 lb) loaf tin and transfer to the middle shelf of a preheated oven, 200°C (400°F), Gas Mark 6. Bake for 1 hour, or until the top is golden brown.

2 Meanwhile, season the turkey fillets on both sides, then heat the oil in a heavy-based frying pan and lightly fry the fillets until golden brown. Add the sugar and cranberry juice to the pan, cover, and simmer gently for 15 minutes. Add the cranberries and cook for a further 5 minutes, or until the turkey has cooked through and the berries have slightly softened.

3 Remove the cooked stuffing from the loaf tin and cut it into 8 thick slices. Remove the turkey fillets from the pan with a slotted spoon; leave them whole or slice them thickly, as you prefer. Keep the stuffing and turkey warm while finishing the sauce. Bring the sauce in the pan to the boil and cook for 5 minutes, or until thickened.

4 Put 2 slices of the stuffing on each of 4 warmed plates and sit the turkey fillets on them. Pour the sauce over the turkey, garnish with thyme and serve at once, with mangetout, if liked.

4 turkey breast fillets, about 150 g (5 oz) each

½ tablespoon vegetable oil

1 tablespoon sugar

300 ml (½ pint) cranberry juice

25 g (1 oz) cranberries, defrosted if frozen

salt and pepper

thyme sprig, to garnish

**Stuffing**:

1 large onion, finely chopped

1 tablespoon vegetable oil

500 g (1 lb) turkey breast meat, minced

50 g (2 oz) fresh white breadcrumbs

175 g (6 oz) canned chestnuts, chopped

25 g (1 oz) dried cranberries

1 teaspoon chopped thyme

2 teaspoons chopped sage

1 egg, beaten

| Serves 4 |
| --- |
| **Preparation time:** 20 minutes |
| **Cooking time:** 1¼ hours |
| kcal 424; kJ 1787; **protein** 64 g; **fat** 9 g; **CHO** 24 g |

1 Place the bulgar wheat in a bowl, add enough cold water to cover, then leave to stand for 30 minutes, until all the water has been absorbed. Line a colander with muslin or a clean tea towel. Drain the bulgar wheat into the colander, then gather up the sides of the cloth or towel and squeeze to extract as much of the liquid as possible. Tip the bulgar wheat into a salad bowl.

2 Stir in the fennel, onion, mint, parsley, fennel seeds, oil, lemon rind and half the lemon juice. Season to taste with salt and pepper. Cover and set aside for 30 minutes, then taste the salad and add more lemon juice, if required.

250 g (8 oz) bulgar wheat

1 fennel bulb, very finely sliced

1 red onion, finely sliced

5 tablespoons chopped mint

5 tablespoons chopped parsley

2 tablespoons fennel seeds, crushed

2 tablespoons olive oil

finely grated rind and juice of 2 lemons

salt and pepper

**Serves 6**

**Preparation time:** 35 minutes, plus soaking

kcal 199; kJ 830; protein 5 g; fat 5 g; CHO 35 g

# tabbouleh & fennel salad

# spaghetti with three herb sauce

1 Put the parsley, tarragon, basil, olive oil, garlic, chicken stock, white wine and salt and pepper to taste into a food processor or liquidizer and purée until smooth.

2 Bring a large saucepan of lightly salted water to the boil, add the spaghetti and cook for 10–12 minutes, or until just tender.

3 Drain the spaghetti well and turn it into a warmed serving bowl; pour over the herb sauce and toss well. Serve immediately.

3 tablespoons chopped parsley

1 tablespoon chopped tarragon

2 tablespoons chopped basil

1 tablespoon olive oil

1 large garlic clove, crushed

4 tablespoons Chicken Stock (see page 8)

2 tablespoons dry white wine

375 g (12 oz) multi-coloured dried spaghetti

salt and pepper

| Serves 4 |
| --- |
| **Preparation time:** 15 minutes |
| **Cooking time:** 10–12 minutes |
| kcal 317; **kJ** 1343; **protein** 12 g; **fat** 5 g; **CHO** 58 g |

# pasta with spring vegetables

1 Cook the broccoli and carrots in lightly salted boiling water for 5–7 minutes until they are tender but still crunchy. Remove with a slotted spoon and drain. Add the petits pois to the water and bring back to the boil. Simmer for 3–4 minutes. Drain well.

2 Bring a large saucepan of lightly salted water to the boil. Add the penne, stir and cook for 10–12 minutes until just tender.

3 Meanwhile, place the mushrooms, wine and parsley in a saucepan and season with salt and pepper. Cook for 8–10 minutes, stirring. Add the cooked vegetables and toss over a high heat to heat through.

4 Drain the penne thoroughly and turn into a warmed bowl. Add the yogurt and vegetables and toss quickly together. Divide the pasta among 4 warmed soup bowls. Sprinkle the Parmesan on top and serve at once.

200 g (7 oz) broccoli florets, divided into tiny sprigs

4 young carrots, thinly sliced

200 g (7 oz) frozen petits pois

375 g (12 oz) dried penne

200 g (7 oz) small button mushrooms, quartered

6 tablespoons dry white wine

2 tablespoons finely chopped parsley

300 ml (½ pint) low-fat natural yogurt

1 tablespoon freshly grated Parmesan cheese

salt and pepper

| Serves 4 |
| --- |
| **Preparation time:** 30 minutes |
| **Cooking time:** 20–25 minutes |
| kcal 457; kJ 1940; protein 24 g; fat 4 g; CHO 83 g |

melon & raspberries in sauternes •

gooseberry & elderflower jelly •

cranberry ice •

lemon honey granita •

melon ice cream •

pear cômpote with chocolate sauce •

hot spiced peaches •

tangerines with cranberry syrup •

strawberry terrine •

figs in sherried yogurt •

summer pudding •

brandy snap waves •

banana & apple slices •

french apple flan •

# sweet nothings

# melon & raspberries in sauternes

1 Halve the melon and either scoop out small balls using a melon baller or a teaspoon or cut the flesh into small cubes.

2 Divide the melon and raspberries among 4 glass dishes. Pour over any melon juice, cover and chill in the refrigerator for at least 2 hours.

3 Just before serving, pour some of the Sauternes into each dish to almost cover the fruit. Serve at once.

1 small ripe Galia melon

175 g (6 oz) fresh or thawed frozen raspberries

½ bottle Sauternes, chilled

**Serves 4**

**Preparation time:** 10 minutes, plus chilling

**kcal** 120; **kJ** 500; **protein** 1 g; **fat** 0 g; **CHO** 12 g

low fat

# gooseberry & elderflower jelly

1 Put the gooseberries into a pan with 300 ml (½ pint) of the apple juice and the elderflower heads, tied in muslin. Cover and cook gently, until the gooseberries are soft. Remove the elderflower heads, squeezing out as much juice as possible.

2 Purée the fruit in a food processor or liquidizer and sieve to remove the tops and tails. Add the sugar and stir until dissolved, then set aside 75 ml (3 fl oz) of the purée.

3 Put the remaining apple juice into a small pan, sprinkle over the agar agar powder, and leave to soak for 5 minutes. Bring to the boil and simmer for 3–4 minutes, until dissolved, then add to the gooseberry purée. Turn into six 125 ml (4 fl oz) decorative moulds and chill until set.

4 To make the sauce, mix the cream with the reserved gooseberry purée. Turn the jellies out on to serving plates, surround each with some sauce, and decorate with the leaves or elderflower sprigs.

500 g (1 lb) gooseberries

450 ml (¾ pint) apple juice

4 elderflower heads

75 g (3 oz) caster sugar

1 teaspoon agar agar powder

75 ml (3 fl oz) single cream

6 fresh edible leaves or elderflower sprigs, to decorate

**Serves 6**

**Preparation time:** 10 minutes

**Cooking time:** 10–15 minutes

**kcal** 136; **kJ** 577; **protein** 1 g; **fat** 3 g; **CHO** 29 g

# cranberry ice

1 Put the cranberry juice and sugar into a saucepan and heat gently to dissolve the sugar completely. Bring to the boil and simmer for 5 minutes. Remove from the heat, stir in the cranberries and orange rind and allow the mixture to cool completely.

2 Pour the mixture into a shallow container and place in the freezer until firm 2.5 cm (1 inch) around the edges. Turn the semi-frozen ice into a bowl, whisk well to break up the ice crystals, then return to the container and freeze until semi-frozen. Whisk once more, then freeze again until firm. Alternatively, pour the chilled mixture into an ice-cream machine and churn until thick and frozen. Transfer to a container and freeze until firm.

3 Remove the cranberry ice from the freezer 15 minutes before serving and scoop it into bowls. Decorate with mint sprigs and sugar-frosted cranberries.

375 ml (13 fl oz) cranberry juice

90 g (3½ oz) caster sugar

125 g (4 oz) cranberries, defrosted if frozen

3 tablespoons finely grated orange rind

**To Decorate:**

mint sprigs

sugar-frosted cranberries (see Cook's Tip)

| Serves 4 |
| --- |
| **Preparation time:** 10 minutes, plus freezing |
| **Cooking time:** 10 minutes |
| kcal 110; **kJ** 470; **protein** 0 g; **fat** 0 g; **CHO** 29 g |

■ To make sugar-frosted cranberries, dip washed and dried cranberries into lightly beaten egg white, then roll them in caster sugar. Set aside on kitchen paper to dry.

1  Cut a slice from the base of each lemon, checking that you leave the side of the fruit, which enables it to stand upright, intact. Slice off the top of each lemon and reserve. Carefully scoop out all the pulp and juice with a teaspoon; do this over a bowl so that no juice is wasted. Discard any white pith, skin and pips from the fruit. Sieve or liquidize the pulp and juice. You need 150 ml (¼ pint). If there is less, make up the quantity with water. Cut out excess pith from the lemon shells and from the tops, being careful not to break the skins.

2  Put the 4 tablespoons of water into a pan with the honey, sugar and bay leaf or lemon balm. Stir over a low heat until the sugar has dissolved, then leave to cool. Blend with the lemon purée and the yogurt or fromage frais. Do not remove the herb at this stage.

3  Pour into a freezing tray or shallow dish and leave until lightly frozen, then gently fork the mixture and remove the herb. Re-freeze the granita for a short time, until it is sufficiently firm to spoon into the lemon shells. Replace the tops of the lemons and put the fruit in the freezer.

4  Transfer the granita-filled lemons to the refrigerator about 20 minutes before serving. Serve decorated with sprigs of lemon balm.

# lemon honey granita

4 large or 6 medium lemons

about 4 tablespoons water

2 tablespoons clear honey

50 g (2 oz) caster sugar

1 bay leaf or 1 lemon balm sprig

450 ml (¾ pint) low-fat natural yogurt or fromage frais

lemon balm sprigs, to decorate

---

**Serves 4–6**

**Preparation time:** 20 minutes, plus cooling and freezing

**kcal** 174; **kJ** 740; **protein** 6 g; **fat** 1 g; **CHO** 38 g

1 Halve the melon and scoop out all the seeds. Scoop the melon flesh into a food processor or liquidizer and blend until smooth.

2 Mix the melon purée with the yogurt. Pour the mixture into a shallow freezer container and freeze until it is firm. Serve the melon ice cream in scoops.

1 large melon (Ogen or Charentais)

300 ml (½ pint) low-fat natural yogurt

| Serves 4 |
| --- |
| **Preparation time:** 20–25 minutes, plus freezing |
| **kcal** 66; **kJ** 278; **protein** 5 g; **fat** 1 g; **CHO** 11 g |

# melon ice cream

# pear compôte with chocolate sauce

1 Peel the pears, leaving the stalks attached and the pears whole. Brush with the lemon juice. Put the sugar in a large saucepan with the water. Heat gently, stirring, until the sugar is completely dissolved. Bring to the boil and boil for 2 minutes. Add the pears, lemon rind, cinnamon stick pieces and cloves. Cover the pan and simmer gently for about 20 minutes, turning once, until the pears are soft.

2 Drain the pears and put them in a serving dish. Measure out 125 ml (4 fl oz) of the syrup and reserve. Add the kirsch to the remaining syrup and pour over the pears.

3 To make the sauce, put the chocolate in a heatproof bowl over a pan of hot water and leave until melted. Put the egg yolks in a large heatproof bowl with the cocoa powder. Whisk until well mixed, then place the bowl over a pan of simmering water and continue whisking, gradually adding the reserved syrup until foamy. Add the melted chocolate and whisk lightly to combine. Serve warm with the pears.

12 small or 6 large ripe pears

2 tablespoons lemon juice

150 g (5 oz) caster sugar

600 ml (1 pint) cold water

2 strips pared lemon rind

1 cinnamon stick, halved

6 cloves

4 tablespoons kirsch

### Sauce:

50 g (2 oz) plain chocolate, broken into pieces

3 egg yolks

1 tablespoon cocoa powder

**Serves 6**

**Preparation time:** 25 minutes

**Cooking time:** about 30 minutes

kcal 302; **kJ** 1274; **protein** 3 g; **fat** 6 g; **CHO** 60 g

4 large ripe fresh peaches

grated rind of 1 lemon

¼ teaspoon ground cinnamon

2 tablespoons clear honey

15 g (½ oz) butter

low-fat fromage frais, to serve
(optional)

1 First skin the peaches. Dip them one at a time into boiling water and slide off the skins. Cut each peach in half, twist to separate the halves, then remove the stone.

2 Arrange the peach halves cut side up in an ovenproof dish. Sprinkle with the lemon rind and cinnamon, then spoon the honey over.

3 Place a dot of butter in the cavity of each peach, cover the dish and bake in a preheated oven, 180°C (350°F), Gas Mark 4, for 15–20 minutes or until the peaches are tender and juicy. Serve hot with low-fat fromage frais, if liked.

| Serves 4 |
| --- |
| **Preparation time:** 5 minutes |
| **Cooking time:** 15–20 minutes |
| kcal 135 **kJ** 572; **protein** 2 g; **fat** 3 g; **CHO** 27 g |

■ Nectarines are also good baked this way. They do not need to be peeled before cooking.

# hot spiced peaches

# tangerines with cranberry syrup

1 Put the sugar and water in a saucepan and heat gently until the sugar has dissolved. Bring to the boil and continue to boil for 5 minutes until the syrup becomes a golden caramel. Put the base of the pan into cold water to stop the caramel darkening further.

2 Add the cranberry juice to the pan and heat gently to dissolve the caramel into the cranberry juice.

3 Remove the skin and pith from the tangerines. Using a sharp knife, cut the pith from the rind of two of the tangerines then cut the rind into narrow strips. Add these to the caramel with the peeled tangerines and gently simmer in a covered pan for 10–15 minutes, turning frequently. Do not overcook.

4 Remove the tangerines from the syrup. Bring the syrup to the boil and continue boiling for 10 minutes, or until thickened. Add the fresh cranberries, remove from the heat, cool, and add the orange liqueur. Pour over the tangerines and chill until required. Serve decorated with a mint sprig.

50 g (2 oz) sugar

125 ml (4 fl oz) water

125 ml (4 fl oz) cranberry juice

8 large tangerines

25 g (1 oz) fresh cranberries

3 tablespoons orange liqueur

mint sprigs, to decorate

**Serves 4**

**Preparation time:** 25 minutes, plus chilling

**Cooking time:** 30–35 minutes

kcal 150; **kJ** 637; **protein** 2 g; **fat** 0 g; **CHO** 32 g

# strawberry terrine

1 Put the gelatine and 3 tablespoons of the water into a small bowl and set aside for 1 minute. Stand the bowl in a pan of hot water and leave until the gelatine has dissolved, about 2 minutes. In a separate bowl, mix the orange juice with the remaining water and the Grand Marnier. Add the dissolved gelatine to the mixture, stirring until well blended. Chill in the refrigerator until the mixture starts to turn syrupy.

2 Lightly oil a 1 kg (2 lb) loaf tin or terrine. Spoon a little of the syrupy jelly over the base and sides of the tin or terrine and line with mint leaves; chill in the freezer briefly.

3 Mix the remaining jelly with the sliced strawberries and spoon into the prepared tin or terrine. Chill in the refrigerator until firm enough to cut. Carefully unmould the terrine and cut into slices. Place each one on a dessert plate and decorate with fanned-out strawberries, strips of orange rind, if liked, and mint or basil sprigs.

5 teaspoons powdered gelatine

300 ml (½ pint) water

300 ml (½ pint) orange juice

2 tablespoons Grand Marnier

handful of large mint leaves

450 g (1 lb) fresh strawberries, hulled and sliced

**To Decorate:**

6 whole strawberries, hulled and sliced

thin strips of orange peel

small mint or basil sprigs

**Serves 4**

**Preparation time:** 30 minutes, plus chilling

**kcal** 58; **kJ** 244; **protein** 2 g; **fat** 0 g; **CHO** 10 g

# figs in sherried yogurt

1 Make a criss-cross cut in the top of each fig and open each one out slightly. Mix the pistachios, apricots, spice and orange rind together and press some of the mixture into the centre of each fig.

2 Mix the yogurt with the sherry and put a spoonful on to 4 dessert plates; carefully arrange 3 stuffed figs on each plate. Scatter the split pistachios over the top and serve, with strips of orange rind arranged at the edge of each plate.

12 fresh figs

3 tablespoons chopped, shelled pistachios

6 dried apricots, finely chopped

pinch of mixed spice

1 teaspoon grated orange rind

6 tablespoons low-fat yogurt

1 tablespoon medium-dry sherry

**To Decorate:**

split pistachios

thin strips of orange rind

**Serves 4**

**Preparation time:** 15–20 minutes

**kcal** 180; **kJ** 768; **protein** 8 g; **fat** 5 g; **CHO** 26 g

# summer pudding

1 Place all the fruit in a large saucepan with the honey and cook very gently for 2–3 minutes, just long enough to soften the fruit and allow the juices to run a little. Sprinkle the gelatine over, if using, and stir it in very carefully, trying not to crush the fruit.

2 Line a lightly greased 1.2 litre (2 pint) pudding basin with three-quarters of the bread, trimming the slices to fit, making certain that all the surfaces are completely covered and the base has an extra thick layer.

3 Spoon in all the fruit, reserving 2 tablespoons of the juice in case the bread is not completely covered when the pudding is taken out. Lay a plate or saucepan lid that will fit inside the rim of the bowl on top and place a 1 kg (2 lb) weight over it. Chill for 10–12 hours. Turn the pudding out on to a plate and cut into wedges to serve.

250 g (8 oz) red and white currants

125 g (4 oz) blackcurrants

125 g (4 oz) raspberries

125 g (4 oz) loganberries

125 g (4 oz) strawberries

125 g (4 oz) cherries, blueberries or cultivated blackberries

1 tablespoon clear honey

1 sachet gelatine (optional)

margarine, for greasing

8 x 1 cm (½ inch) thick slices brown bread, crusts removed (see method)

**Serves 4**

**Preparation time:** 30 minutes, plus chilling

**Cooking time:** 2–3 minutes

kcal 150; kJ 620; protein 5 g; fat 1 g; CHO 30 g

# brandy snap waves

1 Line 2 baking sheets with nonstick greaseproof paper. Arrange 3 wooden spoons on a work surface, parallel to each other with a 1 cm (½ inch) space between each.

2 Sift the flour and ginger on to greaseproof paper. Heat the butter, sugar and syrup in a saucepan until the butter melts. Remove from the heat and stir in the flour mixture and brandy. Mix to a smooth paste.

3 Place 3 dessertspoonfuls of the mixture, spaced well apart, on a baking sheet and bake in a preheated oven, 190°C (375°F), Gas Mark 5, for 6–8 minutes until the biscuits have spread to a lacy texture. Remove from the oven, leave for a few seconds on the baking sheet, then lift the biscuits with a palette knife. Drape them over the spoon handles, pressing down between them so that the biscuits become wavy. Make 4 more batches of brandy snaps in the same way.

4 Put the chocolate in a heatproof bowl over a pan of hot water to melt. Dip the edges of the biscuits in the chocolate and leave to set on a greaseproof paper-lined tray.

75 g (3 oz) plain flour

1 teaspoon ground ginger

75 g (3 oz) unsalted butter

75 g (3 oz) caster sugar

3 tablespoons golden syrup

2 tablespoons brandy

75 g (3 oz) plain chocolate, broken into pieces

| | |
|---|---|
| **Makes** about 15 | |
| **Preparation time:** 25 minutes | |
| **Cooking time:** about 40 minutes | |

kcal 120; **kJ** 506; **protein** 1 g; **fat** 6 g; **CHO** 17 g

# banana & apple slices

1 Grease and line an 18 x 28 cm (7 x 11 inch) shallow baking tin. Cream the margarine and sugar together until light and fluffy. Beat in the eggs one at a time, adding a tablespoon of flour with the second egg. Fold in half the remaining flour with the apples, bananas and sultanas. Fold in the remaining flour with the apple juice.

2 Turn the mixture into the tin and smooth the top with a palette knife. Transfer to a preheated oven, 180°C (350°F), Gas Mark 4, and bake for 45–50 minutes, until the cake springs back when lightly pressed.

3 Turn the cake out on to a wire rack to cool, then sprinkle with the chopped cashew nuts. Cut it into slices to serve.

125 g (4 oz) soft margarine

150 g (5 oz) soft brown sugar

2 eggs

275 g (9 oz) wholemeal self-raising flour

2 dessert apples, cored and grated

2 bananas, mashed

75 g (3 oz) sultanas

125 ml (4 fl oz) apple juice

2 tablespoons chopped cashew nuts

| **Makes:** 20 slices |
| --- |
| **Preparation time:** 20–25 minutes |
| **Cooking time:** 45–50 minutes |
| kcal 158; kJ 666; **protein** 3 g; **fat** 7 g; **CHO** 24 g |

■ The slices freeze well. Pack them into a rigid, freezer container, cover and freeze. They will keep for up to 3 months. To defrost, remove as many as required and leave at room temperature for 1 hour.

# french apple flan

1 To make the pastry, sift the flour on to a cool work surface. Make a well in the centre and add the butter, sugar, egg and egg white and vanilla essence. Using the fingertips of one hand, work these ingredients together, then draw in the flour. Knead lightly until smooth, then cover and chill for 1 hour.

2 Roll out the pastry very thinly on a floured work surface and use to line a 25 cm (10 inch) fluted flan ring. Fill the case generously with the apple purée, then arrange an overlapping layer of apples on top. Sprinkle with the sugar. Bake in a preheated oven, 190°C (375°F), Gas Mark 5, for 35–40 minutes.

3 When the flan is almost cooked, heat the jam with the lemon juice, then strain and brush over the apples while they are still hot. Serve the flan hot or cold.

**Pastry:**

150 g (5 oz) plain flour

50 g (2 oz) butter

50 g (2 oz) caster sugar

1 egg and 1 egg white, beaten together

few drops of vanilla essence

**Filling:**

1 kg (2 lb) cooking apples, peeled, cored, thinly sliced and puréed

2 red-skinned dessert apples, thinly sliced

50 g (2 oz) caster sugar

4 tablespoons apricot jam

juice of ½ lemon

| |
|---|
| **Serves 10** |
| **Preparation time:** 30 minutes, plus chilling |
| **Cooking time:** 35–40 minutes |
| kcal 211; **kJ** 889; **protein** 3 g; **fat** 5 g; **CHO** 41 g |

■ There is no need to grease tins when cooking this type of sweet pastry, called 'pâte sucrée' in France, because of the fat content of the dough.

# index

low fat